Grandmothers

A
TOKEN
· of ·
LOVE

ARIEL BOOKS

Andrews and McMeel
Kansas City

THIS BOOK BELONGS TO

_____

The art of being wise
is the art of knowing
what to overlook.

—WILLIAM JAMES

Common sense,
in an uncommon degree,
is what the world
calls wisdom.

—SAMUEL TAYLOR COLERIDGE

CONTENTS

Introduction · 6

The Family Tree · 9

Family Love · 17

Wisdom & Strength · 25

Kindness & Generosity · 31

A Virtuous Woman · 37

Always A Mother · 45

Raising Grandchildren · 51

Home · 59

The Woman We Love · 73

· 5 ·

Introduction

Grandmothers are
a vital source of wisdom
and tradition, the stable cen-
ter that holds while all around
is in flux. Indeed, with the rapid
changes in American society over
the past decades, grandmothers
have never been more important to
us. They are providers of comfort

and continuity. They teach us how
to live and how to be happy—
and sometimes, if we are good,
they bake us cookies.

This collection of quotes and
poetry reflects the role grandmothers play in our families: the
bond they provide to our past,
and the guidance they give us
for the future.

Such as we are made of,
such we be.

—WILLIAM SHAKESPEARE

You don't choose your family.
They are God's gift to you,
as you are to them.

—DESMOND TUTU

The family is the first essential cell
of human society.

—POPE JOHN XXIII

The family is the association
established by nature
for the satisfaction of man's
everyday wants.

—ARISTOTLE

No matter how many
communes anybody invents,
the family always creeps back.

—MARGARET MEAD

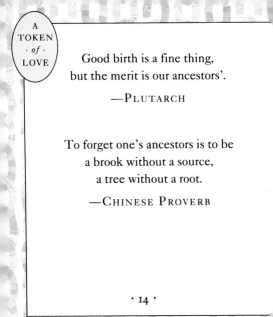

Good birth is a fine thing,
but the merit is our ancestors'.

—PLUTARCH

To forget one's ancestors is to be
a brook without a source,
a tree without a root.

—CHINESE PROVERB

Birth is nothing without virtue,
and we have no claim to share
in the glory of our ancestors
unless we strive to
resemble them.

—MOLIÈRE

Family Love

There is no vocabulary
For the love within a family, love
   that's lived in
But not looked at, love within
   the light of which
All else is seen, the love within
   which
All other love finds speech.
This love is silent.

—T.S. ELIOT

We should measure affection
not like youngsters, by the
ardor of its passion,
but by its strength
and constancy.

—CICERO

If you want to be loved,
be lovable.

—OVID

Love is, above all,
the gift of oneself.

—JEAN ANOUILH

You don't have to go looking
for love when it's where
you come from.

—WERNER ERHARD

Love is never having to say
you're sorry.

—ERIC SEGAL

For finally, we are as we love.
It is love that measures our stature.

—WILLIAM SLOANE COFFIN

The one thing we never give
enough of is love.

—HENRY MILLER

Age doesn't protect you from love.
But love, to some extent,
does protect you from age.

—JEANNE MOREAU

Nothing is so strong
as gentleness,
and nothing so gentle
as real strength.

—ST. FRANCIS DE SALES

Through wisdom
a house is built and
through understanding
it is established.

—PROVERBS 24:3

When our knowledge
coalesces with our humanity
and our humor,
it can add up to wisdom.

—CAROL ORLOCK

Kindness & Generosity

The only gift is a portion
of thyself.

—RALPH WALDO EMERSON

A gift, with a kind countenance,
is a double present.

—THOMAS FULLER

Benevolence is the
characteristic element of
humanity and the great exercise
of it is in loving relatives.

—Tze-Sze

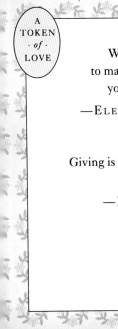

When you cease
to make a contribution,
you begin to die.

—ELEANOR ROOSEVELT

Giving is the highest expression
of potency.

—ERICH FROMM

A kind heart is a fountain
of gladness, making
everything in its vicinity
freshen into smiles.

—WASHINGTON IRVING

A
TOKEN
· of ·
LOVE

Messenger of sympathy
and love, servant of parted
friends, consoler of the lonely,
bond of the scattered family,
enlarger of the common life.

—U.S. POST OFFICE
INSCRIPTION,
Washington, D.C.

Forgiveness is the answer
to the child's dream of a miracle
by which what is broken is
made whole again,
what is soiled is again
made clean.

—DAG HAMMERSKJÖLD

Patience makes a woman
beautiful in middle age.

—ELLIOT PAUL

The true way of softening
one's troubles is to solace
those of others.

—MADAME DE MAINTENON

To feel, to love, to suffer,
and to devote herself
will always be the text
of a woman's life.

—HONORÉ DE BALZAC

Who can find a virtuous woman?
For her price is far above
rubies.
The heart of her husband doth
safely trust in her, so that he
shall not need of spoil.
She will do him good and not evil
all the days of her life.
She stretcheth out her hand to
the poor; yea, she reacheth
forth her hands to the needy.
Strength and honor are her

clothing; and she shall rejoice
in time to come.

She openeth her mouth with
wisdom; and in her tongue is
the law of kindness.

She looketh well to the ways of
her household, and eateth not
the bread of idleness.

Her children arise up, and call
her blessed; her husband also,
and he praiseth her.

—PROVERBS 31:10-12,
19,25-28

Always A Mother

When God thought of Mother,
he must have laughed
with satisfaction, and
framed it quickly—
so rich, so deep, so divine,
so full of soul, power, and beauty,
was the conception.

—HENRY WARD BEECHER

Children are the anchors that
hold a mother to life.

—SOPHOCLES

Mother is the name for God
in the lips and hearts
of children.

—WILLIAM MAKEPEACE
THACKERAY

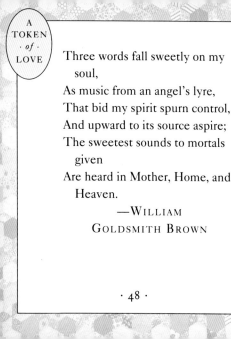

Three words fall sweetly on my
soul,
As music from an angel's lyre,
That bid my spirit spurn control,
And upward to its source aspire;
The sweetest sounds to mortals
given
Are heard in Mother, Home, and
Heaven.

—WILLIAM
GOLDSMITH BROWN

· 48 ·

A mother is not a person
to lean on, but a person to make
leaning unnecessary.

—DOROTHY CANFIELD FISHER

A mother who is really a mother
is never free.

—HONORÉ DE BALZAC

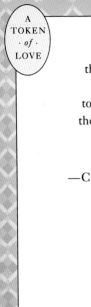

By the time
the youngest children
have learned
to keep the house tidy,
the oldest grandchildren
are on hand
to tear it to pieces.

—CHRISTOPHER MORLEY

Just about the time
a woman thinks her work is done,
she becomes a grandmother.

—ANONYMOUS

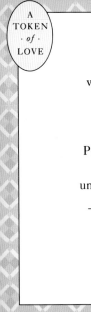

To reform a man,
you must begin
with his grandmother.

—VICTOR HUGO

Perfect love sometimes
does not come
until the first grandchild.

—WELSH PROVERB

Train up a child in the way
he should go; and when he is old,
he will not depart from it.

—PROVERBS 22: 6

Reasoning with a child
is fine if you can reach
the child's reason
before losing your own.

—JOHN MASON BROWN

I looked on child rearing not only
as a work of love and duty, but as
a profession that was fully as in-
teresting and challenging as any
honorable profession in the world
and one that demanded the best
that I could bring to it.

—ROSE KENNEDY,
Grandmother

The reason that grandparents
and grandchildren get along
so well is that they have
a common enemy.

—Sam Levenson

Have children while your parents
are still young enough
to take care of them.

—Rita Rudner

Home

There is nothing like staying
at home for real comfort.

—JANE AUSTEN

I value this delicious home feeling
as one of the choicest gifts
a parent can bestow.

—WASHINGTON IRVING

Half to forget the wandering and
   pain,
Half to remember days that have
   gone by,
And dream and dream that I am
   home again!

—JAMES ELORY FLECKER

If you wanted to gather up all tender memories, all lights and shadows of the heart, all banquetings and reunions, all filial, fraternal, paternal, conjugal affections, and had only just four letters with which to spell out the height and depth and length and breadth and magnitude and eternity of meaning, you would write it out with these four capital letters: HOME.

—DEWITT TALMADGE

· 62 ·

Many make the household but
only one the home.

—JAMES RUSSELL LOWELL

Home is the place where,
when you have to go there,
they have to take you in.

—ROBERT FROST

I gaze on the moon as I tread the
   drear wild,
And feel that my mother now
   thinks of her child,
As she looks on that moon from
   our own cottage door
Thro' the woodbine, whose fra-
   grance shall cheer me no more.
Home, home, sweet, sweet
   home!
There's no place like home, oh,
   there's no place like home.
To thee I'll return,

· 64 ·

overburdened with care;
The heart's dearest solace will
    smile on me there;
No more from that cottage again
    will I roam;
Be it ever so humble, there's no
    place like home.
Home, home, sweet, sweet
    home!
There's no place like home, oh,
    there's no place like home.

—JOHN HOWARD PAYNE

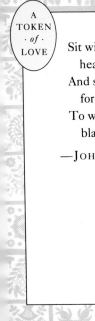

Sit with me at the homestead
   hearth,
And stretch the hands of memory
   forth,
To warm them at the wood-fire's
   blaze.

—JOHN GREENLEAF WHITTIER

This fond attachment to the
  well-known place
When first we started into life's
  long race,
Maintains its hold with such
  unfailing sway,
We feel it e'en in age, and at our
  latest day.

—WILLIAM COWPER

Home's not merely four square
  walls,
Though with pictures hung and
  gilded;
Home is where Affection calls —
Filled with shrines the Hearth
  had builded!
Home! Go watch the faithful
  dove,
Sailing 'neath the heaven above
  us.
Home is where there's one
  to love!

Home is where there's one to
  love us.
Home's not merely roof and room,
It needs something to endear it;
Home is where the heart can bloom,
Where there's some kind lip to
  cheer it!
What is home with none to meet,
None to welcome, none to greet us?
Home is sweet, and only sweet,
Where there's one we love to
  meet us!

—CHARLES SWAIN

A house is built of logs and stone,
Of tiles and posts and piers,
A home is built of loving deeds
That stand a thousand years.

—VICTOR HUGO

Talk of joy: there may be things
better than beef stew and
baked potatoes and
homemade bread—
there may be.

—DAVID GRAYSON

Her ample gown is of cream-
hued linen:
Her grandsons raised the flax and
her granddaughters spun it
with the distaff and wheel.
The melodious character of the
earth,
The finish beyond which
philosophy cannot go, and
does not wish to go,
The justified mother of men.

—WALT WHITMAN

A beautiful lady
is an accident of nature.
A beautiful old lady
is a work of art.

—LOUIS NIZER

Not to do honor to old age
is to demolish in the morning
the house wherein we are
to sleep at night.

—ALPHONSE KARR

As pure and sweet, her fair brow
   seemed eternal as the sky;
And like the brook's low song,
   her voice, a sound which could
   not die.
Sweet promptings unto kindest
   deeds were in her very look;
We read her face, as one who reads
   a true and holy book.

—JOHN GREENLEAF WHITTIER

Our chief want in life is
somebody who will make us
do what we can.

—RALPH WALDO EMERSON

The Queen Mother…
warm, smiling, human,
understanding, she embodied
everything the public could want
of its grandmother.

—JOHN PEARSON

The woman who creates
and sustains a home,
and under whose hands
children grow up to be strong
and pure men and women
is a creator second
only to God.

—HELEN HUNT JACKSON

The text of this book was
set in Caslon 540
by Beth Tondreau Design
of New York, NY.

Design by Beth Tondreau Design

Calligraphy by Carole Lowenstein